GOOD OL' Cowgirl STORIES

PAINTINGS BY

jackTerry

HARVEST HOUSE PUBLISHERS

EUGENE, OREGON

DEDICATION

To my unforgettable grandmothers:
Maggie Mason, Etna Terry, Airie Herring

To my endearing aunts:
*Velma Jo McCully, Maybelle Mason,
Lauranette Mason, Sonny Mason, Masie Mason,
Dorothy Mills, Wilma Stone*

And especially to my dear mother,
Della Merle Herring

Good Ol' Cowgirl Stories

Artwork copyright © 2007 by Jack Terry and may not be reproduced without the artist's permission. For more information regarding art prints featured in this book, please contact:

Jack Terry Fine Art, Ltd.
100 Olde Oak
Georgetown, TX 78628
512-864-2990

Text by Hope Lyda

Published by Harvest House Publishers
Eugene, Oregon 97402
ISBN-13: 978-0-7369-2023-0
ISBN-10: 0-7369-2023-4

Design and production by Koechel Peterson & Associates, Inc., Minneapolis, Minnesota

Unless otherwise indicated, all Scripture quotations are taken from the Holy Bible, New International Version®. NIV®. Copyright © 1973, 1978, 1984 by the International Bible Society. Used by permission of Zondervan. All rights reserved.

Harvest House Publishers has made every effort to trace the ownership of all poems and quotes. In the event of a question arising from the use of a poem or quote, we regret any error made and will be pleased to make the necessary correction in future editions of this book.

Quote in "What They Wore" and research for "Royalty on the Range" from *Daughters of the West* by Anne Seagraves (Hayden, Idaho: Wesanne Publications, 1996).

For information about the origination of the song "Happy Trails," visit www.cowgirls.com.

Special thanks to Bernard Price for permission to reprint his cowgirl poems *The Cowgirl* and *The Life She Loves.*

Printed in Hong Kong

07 08 09 10 11 12 13 14 15 / NG / 10 9 8 7 6 5 4 3 2 1

CONTENTS

*The history of every country begins
in the heart of a man or a woman.*
WILLA CATHER

VERY EARLY in the creation of all things, God acknowledged man's necessity for a helper. The cowboy has a hard enough time surviving in today's world, and if it weren't for cowgirls, his way of life would probably be extinct.

Cowgirls go way back in my genealogy. These great women struggled to raise their families amid the many hardships of pioneer life. Through droughts, depression, and disease they fought for what they believed in, many times sewing clothes from flour and feed sacks, growing their own food, and cooking on a woodstove. They boiled water to scrub the laundry and even drove a team of mules hundreds of miles in search of greener pastures. They could handle a rope, reigns, and a shotgun as well as a sewing needle, iron skillet, and garden hoe. The most admirable qualities I recall in these great women were their unwavering faith and spiritual leadership that bonded the hearts of their loved ones with their Creator. You see, when a cowgirl sets her mind to do something, it gets done.

"It's all gonna be all right" are words I will never forget from the cowgirls I have loved the most. Always trusting, faithful, and true, they were never afraid to dirty their hands but could look like a million dollars half an hour later just in time for church. Putting others first and usually settling for much less appreciation than they deserved, they always dreamed big, worked hard, and instilled hope for a better future for everyone.

So hats off to all you cowgirls out there. Carry on the great traditions of the ladies in the stories you are about to read and make some new ones of your own. There are a lot of us cowboys out here who are depending on you.

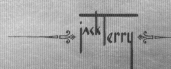

Cowgirl is a condition of the heart.
JOYCE GIBSON ROACH

The Heart
OF A
Cowgirl

THE OPENING up of the West stirred the spirit of hope and discovery in many men and women. They dreamed of looking out over a new horizon. They dreamed of rising before the sun made its showing to serve the land and, in return, to know it would serve them and their families. They dreamed of freedom, space, and possibility. There was risk entering the unknown, but there was also the promise of new beginnings.

Some women held these dreams close to their hearts as they climbed into a wagon, mounted a horse, or paid their fare for the train. Many others agreed to follow and support the dreams of husbands or fathers only to find themselves widowed or orphaned before they arrived at this place of promise. For all these women, their perseverance gave birth to great hope.

Women of the West gained great personal strength and faith as they lived their days in the West. They shared in the taming of the land, but they faced a new frontier that the men did not. They broke through barriers greater than mountain ranges and jumped chasms far deeper than the ravines. In everything they did, they were planting the seeds of "firsts"—the seeds of possibility—that have been harvested by every woman since. They managed ranches; they were resilient partners for their husbands; they raised families; they became doctors, writers, politicians, entrepreneurs, artists, performers, competitors, and legends.

A journey through their stories is not as much about history as it is about the spirit of all women. It is the spirit of the cowgirl in every woman—no, in every person—that exchanges disappointment for faith, regret for hope, and defeat for courage. This is the way of the West. This is the way of dreams. This is the heart of the cowgirl. ❖

I may not dream about being a cowboy
these days, but I have two daughters
and they dream about being a lot of things
I never saw girls doing when I was a boy.
As their father, I want them to be anything
they want to be. And whatever they become,
I'd like them to have an attitude like that of
the cowgirl I mistook for a cowboy: holding the
reins with confidence, sitting deep in the saddle, head
high, in control, female and proud. Like that cowgirl,
I'd like my girls to look toward futures that are big
and open and just this side of being tamed.

MARC TALBERT

Holding the Reins: A Ride Through Cowgirl Life

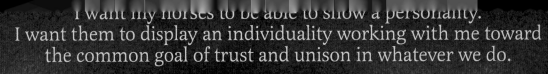

I want my horses to be able to show a personality.
I want them to display an individuality working with me toward
the common goal of trust and unison in whatever we do.

SHERRY CERVI
two-time world champion barrel racer

I work on our family ranch that was settled over one

hundred years ago. Ranching is not an easy life, but it is

intensely rewarding. It can be brutally difficult—physically,

emotionally, and financially—but in the midst of it all is a

powerful spirituality and a sense of being centered and

anchored to the most basic and beautiful things in life....

Ranching means having both roots and wings.

BECKY PRUNTY
Cowgirls in Heaven

Women Firsts
IN THE AMERICAN WEST

- In 1812, Jane Barnes from Portsmouth, England, became the first white woman in the Pacific Northwest when she traveled with Donald McTavish to the North West Company's fur trading post.

- Bethenia Owens-Adair was the first woman doctor in the West. She lived in Oregon.

- Nellie Cashman, a petite Irish girl, became the first female prospector in America.

- Esther Hobart Morris became the United States' first female justice of the peace in 1870. Her efforts led to the right for women to vote in the Wyoming Territory in 1869.

- Clara Brown, an ex-slave, went to Colorado and established the first Sunday school in Denver.

- The first woman entrant in organized rodeo challenged her male competitors before the competition even started. In 1904, a driving rain at the Cheyenne Frontier Days celebration turned the track into a mud pit. The cowboys determined it was too dangerous to ride and asked for a postponement. But the spry and impatient Bertha Kaepernick challenged their hesitation. She even rode a wild horse by the grandstand to prove the track was adequate. Needless to say, the men quickly bucked up.

- Tillie Baldwin was the first female to bulldog steers. She won her first bronc riding contest in 1911. She also won the Roman race against male competitors in 1913. Roman racing required the participant to ride standing with one foot on each of two horses.

- In 1905, Lucille Mulhall was the first woman to be called a "cowgirl."

- Ruth Roach was the first woman to ride a bronc at the Fort Worth Stock Show in 1917.

- At a rodeo show in Fort Worth, Texas, Vera Mac, known as "Little Mac," was the first woman to publicly wear men's trousers. Soon other cowgirls followed suit.

- Bonnie McCarroll made rodeo history in 1922 by winning the Cowgirl Bronc Riding Championship at the two most prestigious rodeos in the nation: Cheyenne Frontier Days and the first Madison Square Garden Rodeo.

- Fox Hastings was one of the few female bulldoggers in rodeo history. Her fastest time was 17 seconds, a record she set in 1924.

- In 1948, women gathered in San Angelo, Texas, to create the Girls Rodeo Association, the first rodeo association just for women.

- Sherry Cervi made history as the world champion barrel racer in 1999. In that one year she made more in rodeo prize money than any other woman or man.

A Great Shot
A GIVING HEART

THE NAME SYNONYMOUS with "cowgirl" is Annie Oakley. This is most appropriate not because of the depictions of her life in the popular musical *Annie Get Your Gun,* but because the real Annie Oakley represented the heart and soul of the true cowgirl.

Annie's perseverance shone brightly throughout her life. After her father passed away and her mother was widowed a second time, Annie was sent to a county poor farm where she was forced into servitude with an abusive family. As soon as she was able, Annie reunited with her mother and siblings, who were struggling to make ends meet.

Young, determined, and a born natural with a gun, Annie took to hunting game for money to become the family's provider. The hunting was not only a wise survival decision, but it led to her fame as a sharpshooter. So great was her reputation that in 1881 when Frank Butler of the Baughman and Butler shooting act came to her area and bet a hotelier $100 that he could out-shoot any local, the local selected was 21-year-old Annie. Butler was amused by his seemingly innocent competitor, but when that petite, young woman beat him, his amusement turned to adoration. They were

married the next year and eventually performed together. Witnessing her skill at a show in 1884, Sitting Bull was impressed by Annie, her stature, and her poise. After numerous conversations, he thought of her as a daughter and nicknamed her "Little Sure Shot," which became her moniker in advertisements and throughout history.

When it became clear that Annie was the true star of the family, Frank stepped behind the scenes to become her business manager. Annie eventually joined Buffalo Bill's famous Wild West Show and was beloved by countless audience members throughout the world including Queen Victoria and the Crown Prince of Germany. Her tricks, such as shooting an apple off the top of her dog's head, were feats that amazed onlookers and garnered her many fans and considerable financial rewards.

The strength of her marriage and of Annie's spirit helped her endure and survive two serious accidents. Despite these trials, Annie set shooting records well into her sixties. She taught women of all ages how to shoot and encouraged women's rights. And just like the girl who found an industrious way to support her family, the older Annie was quick to help others.

Annie embodied the heart of the western woman. She overcame obstacles that would have defeated most others. She is remembered not only for her rise to fame, but also for her desire to rise to the occasion to serve and support friends, family, and strangers—and to take an incredible shot here and there. ❖

Luck is not chance, it's toil.
Fortune's expensive smile
is earned.
EMILY DICKINSON

The Heart

OF A
Cowgirl

Compassion

*Throughout her life, Annie Oakley
reached out to help those in need.
She cared about people, especially children.
Annie made one final act of generosity
shortly before her death.
She had her many silver and gold medals
melted down and gave the money they earned
to a children's charity.*

KATHERINE KROHN
Women of the Wild West

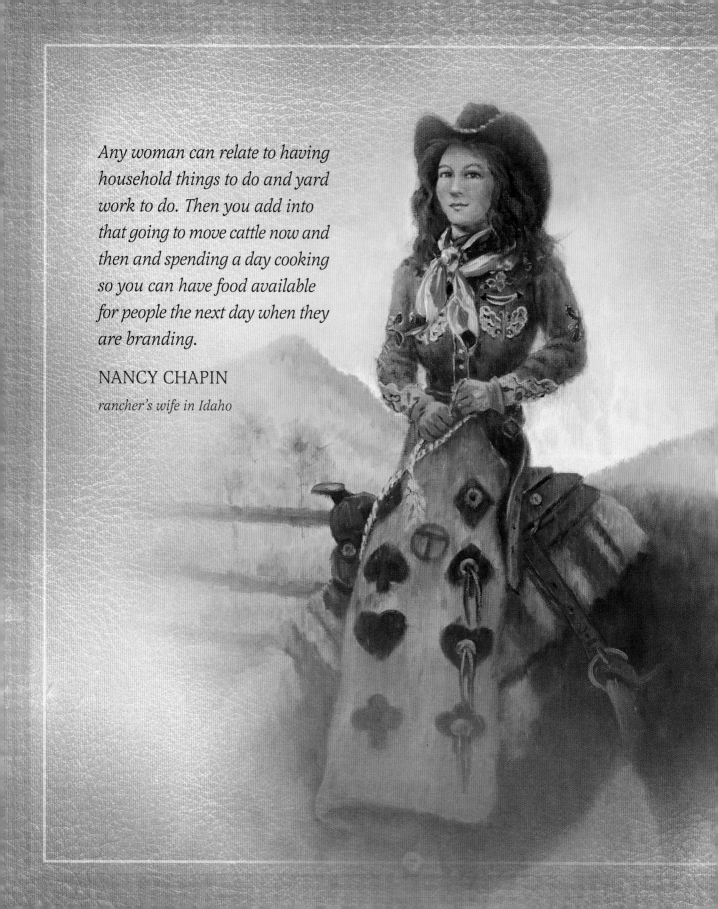

Any woman can relate to having household things to do and yard work to do. Then you add into that going to move cattle now and then and spending a day cooking so you can have food available for people the next day when they are branding.

NANCY CHAPIN

rancher's wife in Idaho

Mother TO ALL

MARY ANN (MOLLY) DYER was a young woman when her parents died, and she took the reins of raising her younger brothers in the late 1850s. While her older brothers fought in the Civil War, she became a teacher to provide financial security for her family. Molly handled the weight of this responsibility with great grace and determination. Later she met and married one of the most well-known ranchers in history, Charles Goodnight. Moved to the huge JA Ranch in Colorado, she took to ranching life with that same grace.

The lack of other females in the area didn't discourage Molly from creating a community. She was a hardworking partner for Charles, and she befriended cowboys, Indians, and the animals of the area. She liked to look out for all of them. When commercial hunters raged their destruction across the Plains, slaughtering buffalo and leaving behind the offspring, Molly rescued the baby buffalos and set aside 150 acres for the Goodnight buffalo herd. She became known worldwide for saving buffalos from extinction.

A devout woman of faith, Molly also set out to save a few souls among the cowboys who worked for her husband and her. She would hold church services and Sunday school sessions. Many cowboys traveled great distances to spend the day with her in the presence of the Lord. It was a time of comfort and community.

Mary went from a life of security with her parents to the hard work of raising her siblings to the many unknowns of being a cattleman's wife. Through it all, her innate nurturing always connected her to those in her charge, and in Molly's heart, that included everyone she met.

We have hard work to do, and loads to lift;
Shun not the struggle—face it;
'tis God's gift.
MALTI BABCOCK

The Heart
OF A
Cowgirl

Partner

Enshrined in the minds and hearts of countless cowboys as the Mother of the Panhandle, Molly became doctor, nurse, homemaker, spiritual comforter, sister, and mother to the hands who worked for her husband.

JOYCE GIBSON ROACH

The Handbook of Texas Online

A woman's work is
always toward wholeness.

MAY SARTON

SOURDOUGH STARTER

Mary Goodnight's husband invented the first chuck wagon. In the chuck wagons or out on the trail, cowgirls and cowboys often dined on breads and biscuits created with sourdough starter. Here is a simple, contemporary recipe for starter.

> ½ cup lukewarm water
> 1 package active dry yeast
> 1 tablespoon sugar
> 2 cups warm tap water
> 2½ cups all-purpose flour

Pour the half cup of warm water into a mixing bowl. Stir in yeast and stir until dissolved. Add the sugar and mix until dissolved. Stir in the other 2 cups of warm water. Gradually add the flour, stirring constantly until smooth. Pour this mixture into a glass jar and place a paper towel over the top. Set the jar in a warm place and stir twice daily for three days (sometimes longer) until bubbles form, which shows the starter is active and working! This can then be stored in the refrigerator, covered with a paper towel secured with a rubber band for two weeks.

GEORGIA'S SOURDOUGH STARTER BISCUITS

1 cup sourdough starter
1 tablespoon oil
1 tablespoon sugar
½ teaspoon salt
1 teaspoon baking soda
1 to 2 cups flour

Preheat oven to 375 degrees. Mix all ingredients except for the flour. Then add 1 to 2 cups flour, being careful to not add too much. The dough will be soft. Knead dough 30 to 60 times. Pat or roll out to ½ inch thick and cut out biscuits with a biscuit cutter. Place biscuits with the sides barely touching on a lightly greased pan. Let rise for 30 minutes. Bake in preheated oven for 10 minutes.

An Original

WHILE OTHER GIRLS in the early 1900s spent their childhoods enjoying the company of dolls and the practice of sewing, young Lucille Mulhall was hanging out with horses and roping rabbits, wolves, and any animals she could find on her family's Oklahoma ranch. Those who wrote off her fascination with training ponies and practicing trick riding moves as the follies of a wild child soon changed their tune. As a mere teenager, Lucille became a top cowboy performer in the West.

Bright, educated, gentle in feminine spirit, and possessing strength well beyond that which her physical stature implied, Lucille was the only woman to rope steers competitively with men. At that point in history, this alone was a feat to take notice of, but it was her infectious passion for the cowboy way of life that won the hearts of anyone fortunate enough to see her skills in action. When she traveled to the East Coast in 1905, ❖

her popularity preceded her, and fans, competitors, and the media struggled to find a way to classify this young female wonder of the roping world. For the first time ever, the term "cowgirl" was coined. Most sources attribute Will Rogers with bestowing the name upon Lucille. He was her teacher and a great admirer of her God-given talent.

Whatever Little Miss Mulhall was called by those in awe of her abilities, she made a name for herself in the annals of history. Her entry with the Cowgirl Hall of Fame in Fort Worth, Texas, states, "Lucille helped make women an integral part of rodeo." With ability, agility, and poise, Lucille changed the face of the Wild West and gave the horse-riding women to follow a name of their very own: Cowgirl.

There's a magical tie to the land of our home,
which the heart cannot break,
though footsteps may roam.
ELIZA COOK

The Heart
OF A
Cowgirl

Boldness

Barbara Inez (Tad) Lucas was fourteen when her brother dared her to ride a steer at a 1916 county fair. The brave girl entered, won, and went on to win the finals. From this defining moment, she became the world's best female rodeo performer of her time. She garnered the major trophies and titles available to rodeo cowgirls and was known as a daring and innovative trick rider.

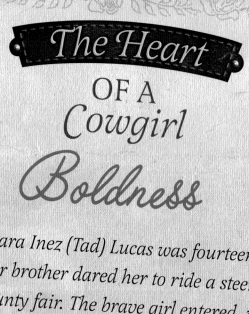

*Boot, saddle, to horse,
and away!*

ROBERT BROWNING

THE
Cowgirl

BERNARD PRICE

A Cowgirl is a special breed
That loves the outdoor life,
She's really not content
Staying home, a rancher's wife.

The cattle and the horses
All the critters that she knows,
Get the care they need.
Her feelings for them shows.

Can turn her hand to anything
Throughout the busy day,
Milking cows or mending fences
Putting up the hay.

Riding with the ranch hands
They work so well together,
Facing all that comes along
In any kind of weather.

Some days ain't so easy
When trouble may arise,
With experience and know-how
To sort it out she tries.

No matter what the problem
They never get her down,
Wouldn't change this lifestyle
For any job in town.

Working dawn 'til dusk
Is the price she's glad to pay,
To own the ranch that shows
How much she does each day.

The life she leads is full
Don't have much time for fun,
Now and then a barn dance
With her man when work is done.

One day she'll look back
And recall the role she played
Thankful for the blessings shared
And every choice she made.

It is not because things are difficult
that we do not dare;
It is because we do not dare
that they are difficult.

SENECA

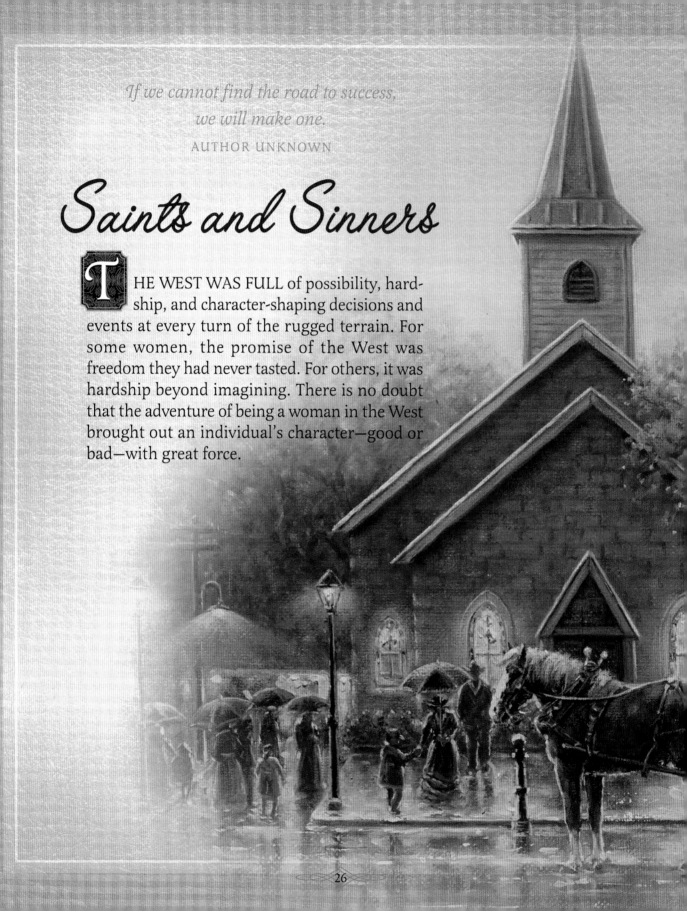

Saints and Sinners

THE WEST WAS FULL of possibility, hardship, and character-shaping decisions and events at every turn of the rugged terrain. For some women, the promise of the West was freedom they had never tasted. For others, it was hardship beyond imagining. There is no doubt that the adventure of being a woman in the West brought out an individual's character—good or bad—with great force.

AMERICA'S WEST held great promise for women around the world. An Irish girl, Nellie Cashman, left Ireland in 1844 and ventured to America. Eventually she ended up in the West and traveled among the mining camps. She was strong in her faith and seemed called to assist wherever and however she could. The pale of Irish skin and her petite frame seemed in contradiction of this remarkable woman's strength. When a group of miners were stricken with scurvy in the far North, Nellie led a group of men with aid supplies through the treacherous area.

In 1882, Nellie owned and operated a hotel and restaurant in the infamous town of Tombstone, Arizona. While living in a town known for scandal, violence, and the roughest men and women of the West, Nellie used her business savvy to hold successful fund-raising drives for various charities. This woman, who was called the Angel of Tombstone, brought three Sisters of Mercy to town in order to run the city and county hospital. And when space was needed, she would transform her hotel into a makeshift hospital to aid the sick. She established the first school in Tombstone. When her beloved sister died, she raised her nieces and nephews and provided for their education.

Unfazed by her surroundings and perhaps even inspired by them, Nellie always shared her light with others. When a man was building grandstands and selling tickets for people to witness the hanging of five men, Nellie made sure the grandstands were torn down. And while talking to the men destined to die, she converted two of them to faith. Nellie eventually left Tombstone when mining dwindled and the promise of more adventure called her to Africa and Alaska.

Nellie didn't round up cattle, but she was a cowgirl through and through. She never shied away from the chance to experience a new frontier.

*Tenacity is when
you follow your heart—
when the whole world
is screaming to get
back into your head.*

SONIA CHOQUETTE

AS THE ANGEL OF TOMBSTONE rounded up funds for the needy or the sick, the "White Devil of the Yellowstone," aka Calamity Jane, aka Martha Jane Canary, was lassoing her share of adventure throughout the West. Just like the tales of many famous men of her time, Calamity Jane's story was buoyed by a lot of myth—a condition she perpetuated with frequent false mentions of rubbing elbows with the most well-known men of the West. For years she claimed to be very close to Bill Hickok when she was not more than an acquaintance.

Ironically, Jane probably could've relied on the facts for her celebrity to prosper. There are numerous tales of her heroic deeds, including a time when the driver of a stagecoach was wounded by an Indian's arrow. As a passenger and witness, Jane quickly climbed to his seat, grabbed the reins, and led the other passengers—six men who had been afraid to step up—to safety. When a smallpox plague afflicted the town of Deadwood, South Dakota, Jane helped nurse many of the citizens to health. This selfless act shaped a legacy of sainthood in that town. Even her nickname was achieved out of a moment of great bravery. Captain Egan had fallen from his horse when he was surrounded by a band of Indians. Without hesitation, Jane rode into the mayhem, pulled the Captain up on her horse, and blazed away, saving them both from the tragic fate of the rest of the company.

While she was a rough character, much of Calamity Jane's reputation came from the advent of the dime novels that spread fabricated stories far and wide about her wildness and that of other colorful personas. The truth behind Jane's bravado was more compelling than any of those novels might have depicted. She had lost her mother when she was little, and at the age of ten she was separated from her brothers and father in an Indian uprising. This young girl was forced to create a life on her own. That demanding requirement created a need for independence as well as a hunger for fame and attention. Calamity Jane achieved both in her unique style. ❖

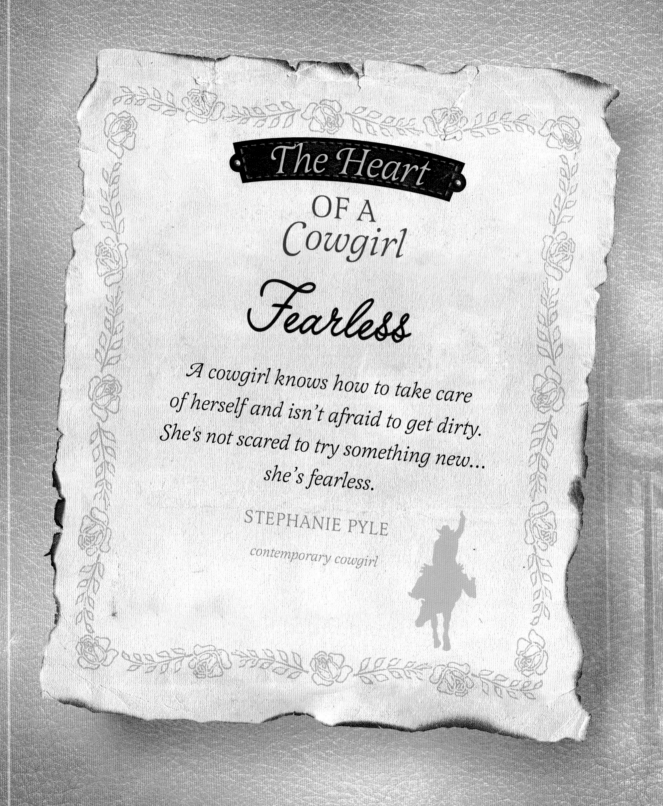

The Heart

OF A
Cowgirl

Fearless

A cowgirl knows how to take care of herself and isn't afraid to get dirty. She's not scared to try something new... she's fearless.

STEPHANIE PYLE

contemporary cowgirl

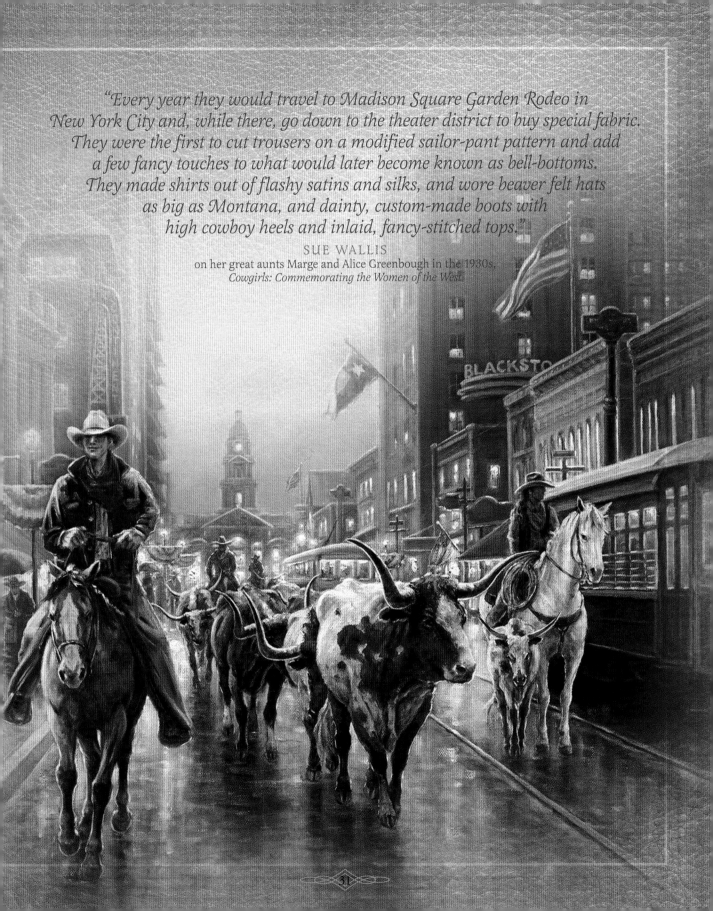

"*Every year they would travel to Madison Square Garden Rodeo in New York City and, while there, go down to the theater district to buy special fabric. They were the first to cut trousers on a modified sailor-pant pattern and add a few fancy touches to what would later become known as bell-bottoms. They made shirts out of flashy satins and silks, and wore beaver felt hats as big as Montana, and dainty, custom-made boots with high cowboy heels and inlaid, fancy-stitched tops.*"

SUE WALLIS
on her great aunts Marge and Alice Greenbough in the 1930s,
Cowgirls: Commemorating the Women of the West.

What They Wore

- In the early 1800s, women wore full-length skirts and tried to maintain both function and propriety.

- By the late 1800s, some women wore split skirts. Sometimes at rodeos and on the range, women would wear skirts over trousers.

- Women in the 1900s wore split skirts or loose trousers.

- With the advent of Wild West shows and female rodeo stars, clothing became much more decorative, flamboyant, and expressive. In 1918, a carefree young woman named Prairie Rose Henderson, who had helped open the gates of rodeo arenas for females ten years earlier, showed up for a 1918 rodeo in Nebraska wearing ostrich plumes over bloomers and a blouse covered with bright sequins. Wherever she went she disregarded what was expected and gave the crowd and the rodeo industry a taste of the true Wild West—fashion style.

- By the time World War II began, women outside the Wild West circuit also let function and a desire for fashion override societal restrictions and many wore pants.

"As was to be expected, all these females had a profound effect upon rodeo costuming. Blue jeans and buckskins were too drab for them; they began wearing red velvet skirts with brilliantly decorated hems, then exchanged the fancy skirts for bright-colored trousers with flaring hips. From there they went to silk shirts of all hues and fancy neckpieces."

DEE BROWN
The Gentle Tamers

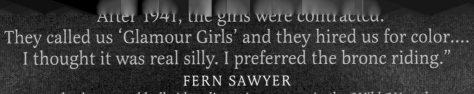

After 1941, the girls were contracted.
They called us 'Glamour Girls' and they hired us for color....
I thought it was real silly. I preferred the bronc riding."
FERN SAWYER
a popular bronc and bull rider, discussing women in the Wild West shows

Royalty
ON THE RANGE

WHILE SOME WOMEN ADJUSTED to the West by becoming rough of exterior and interior, others kept an air of refinement as they made a path through this very male world. Kitty Wilkins was such a woman. When she was young, her family moved from Oregon to Idaho and purchased a large ranch surrounded by the Owyhee Mountains, a roaming ground for many wild horses. The Wilkins family hired buckaroos to catch these horses and then bring them back to the ranch to be tamed and then sold. Kitty broke colts and developed excellent riding skills. When a friend of the family gave her a $20 gold piece, she put her money where her heart and purpose were and invested in a filly. Soon she acquired a herd of more than 700 horses and became actively involved in the family business. Even with her father and three brothers on board, it was clear that she was in charge.

With her stylish clothing, carefully kempt hair, and shrewd business sense, Kitty became known as the "Horse Queen of Idaho." She officially took over the family business in the late 1800s and tasted success for many years. Her business practices included frequent publicity and a

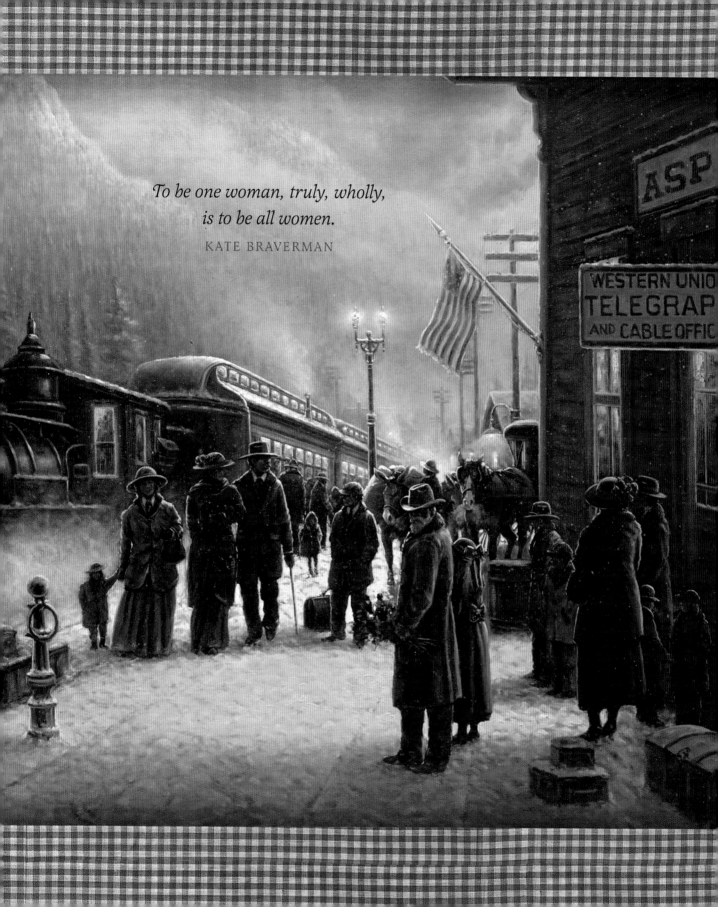

To be one woman, truly, wholly,
is to be all women.

KATE BRAVERMAN

commitment to make the deliveries in person, even when that required long train rides transporting thousands of horses. At the time she was the only female horse trader, so there were many looks of surprise when she went to the stockyards. When men looking for work came to see "Kit," they assumed it was a male employer. Some may have hesitated to work alongside a woman in those days, but as soon as they saw her riding skills and witnessed her strength as a business manager, they typically agreed to stay on for many years. She treated her crew well but would fire them in an instant if they got out of line.

Kitty used her clout to influence many lives for good. She supported an orphanage and a Catholic academy. From these places, she also selected boys to work with her crew and girls to help at her house. A few were even sent on for further education at Kitty's expense. Because of her skill and requirements for discipline, the men who worked and rode with her became top cowboys. Some of them even ended up becoming celebrities in the Wild West show circuit.

Truly a colorful, vibrant, and talented woman, Kitty earned respect everywhere she went. Her call to excellence inspired success in others for years to come.

The Heart

OF A
Cowgirl

Guts

Those days you could do anything
you wanted to
if you were gutsy enough.

MITZI LUCAS RILEY

rodeo trick rider and daughter

of rodeo star Tad Lucas

Happy Tales

DALE EVANS was a woman of great charm and perseverance. She faced personal heartache and the demands of raising a son alone while building her singing career. Blessed with an angelic voice, Dale worked as a singer in various genres of music. Her growing popularity led to film contracts. When she was given a role in *The Cowboy and The Senorita* opposite the dashing Roy Rogers, it was the start of two new trails for her—a significant movie career and the future love of her life. A few years later, Roy and Dale dated and eventually were married in a ceremony at the Flying L Ranch, where they had just finished filming *Home in Oklahoma*.

Most people don't realize that it was Dale who wrote the famous song "Happy Trails." In 1950, Roy was doing the radio show, and Dale felt he needed a theme song, so she started to jot down ideas. Roy often signed autographs with the phrase "happy trails," so Dale used that as a title, and the lyrics quickly followed.

Just before the show was to start, she taught Roy and the Sons of the Pioneers the melody and a trademark was born.

The Rogers knew more than many that success and celebrity did not protect a family from loss and suffering. Their only shared biological daughter, Robin, died before the age of two from complications related to Down's Syndrome. They adopted four children; two were killed in separate, tragic accidents. Through it all, they remained faithful and prayerful and even stronger in their convictions. Over the years, many children, adults, musicians, and actors looked to them as pillars of strength and honor. They were role models because of how they lived even when the cameras weren't rolling.

Dale and Roy had an exceptional business partnership, one of the most successful in history, but their greatest legacy was their devotion to faith and to family and their encouragement of a nation to do the same. ❖

The wildest, most dangerous trails are always the ones within.

BELDEN LAKE

The Heart
OF A
Cowgirl

Role Model

It was not until Dale Evans,
Queen of the West,
joined the King of the Cowboys
that young girls in theater audiences
had a heroine to look up to.

LILLIAN TURNER

Points West, of the Buffalo Bill Historical Center newsletter

Chargin' out the chute
The bronc arena bound,
Its rider loudly hollers
As they go round and round.

Usin' all her know-how
The cowgirl keeps her seat,
When she hears the buzzer
Knows her ride is now complete.

The pick-up men assist
She dismounts and in the clear,
Walks away while wavin'
To the crowd who loudly cheer.

Very happy with the ride
And the prize she's won today,
After she collects her money
Will soon be on her way.

Another rodeo is callin'
It's really all she knows,
With her saddle in the truck
To the next one off she goes.

This life she chose ain't easy
From state to state she'll roam
Her family back in Texas
Wishin' she would come on home.

But somethin' keeps her goin'
The popularity and fame,
Until it's time to quit
And she gives up this game.

When her last ride is over
And the life she loves is through,
Memories help her to endure
She now has quite a few.

Welcomed after years away
A hometown hero still
Her record never matched
And boots so hard to fill.

THE
Life She Loves

BERNARD PRICE

TODAY'S
Cowgirl

THE COWGIRLS OF TODAY are vibrant, creative, surprising, and inspiring. They don't take for granted those first achievements of the women who came before them; instead, they pay homage to those women and their successes in all they do. And like all cowgirls before them, they look beyond what is known to the land of more firsts. They seek a personal best in the rodeo arena, but they also seek a universal best for community, family, society, and world.

Unlike their earlier role models, they know what the geographic landscape looks like. But they are kindred spirits nonetheless because they don't know what lies beyond that next trial, accomplishment, or frontier. They hold the same reverent awe for the unknowns ahead, and they too are up to the challenge.

She is clothed with strength and dignity;
she can laugh at the days to come.

PROVERBS 31:25 NIV

My first horse, Buster, was a Welsh Mountain Pinto pony; he had a spunky side. Every day we had our disagreements... either I ended up walking home alone, or I was riding him back. But the funny thing was, after all of that effort, he'd do anything I asked of him—run through rivers, climb mountains, and once he even climbed stairs to my mother's back porch. I was the only one he'd let ride him; my dad would try and he would buck him off. My sister tried riding him, and he'd buck her off too. We may've had our disagreements, but we loved each other and at the end of the day, we were best of friends.

I've been around horses my entire life. I've showed horses, barrel raced, jumped... I even had a job offer to be a jockey in Canada. Anything you can think of, I've done it, but I'm far from being done. This year I'm going to college in Wyoming to study Equine Riding and Training and Equine Business Management. My goal is to have my own stables to board horses and to give lessons. I want to create a therapy riding program for children with disabilities. I've had the privilege of helping with this kind of program, and the joy on the kids' faces was amazing. There hasn't been a greater joy in my life.

✦ STEPHANIE PYLE, *21-year-old cowgirl*

The best remedy for those
   who are afraid, lonely or unhappy
is to go outside,
   somewhere where they can be quiet,
   alone with the heavens, nature and God.

ANNE FRANK

The Heart
OF A
Cowgirl

Courage

*Everybody has a little
amount of fear...
it's the courage you have to
overcome it that makes it so wonderful,
that makes a successful bull rider.*

LISA STIPP

1998 World Champion bull-rider

Rodeo Drive

odeo was the first sport in which women were allowed to compete against males. Rodeo gave women a chance to earn money and a chance to show what they were made of then and now. In the rodeo arena, women expressed the heart of the cowgirl. These are some of the primary rodeo events for women.

BAREBACK BRONC RIDING: This is a demanding and dangerous event because the rider doesn't use a saddle as she stays on the bucking horse as long as possible. Even while waiting to go out into the arena, a cowgirl must use great strength to control the horse in the chute.

BULL RIDING: A rider holds a bullrope, which is wrapped around her hand and around the bull. Without touching her own body or that of the bull with her free hand, a competitor tries to stay on for eight seconds.

BARREL RACING: Three barrels are placed in a cloverleaf pattern in the arena. Riders enter the area and quickly maneuver around each barrel and then exit. This is a speed event, and every step, turn, and stride matters. There is a five-second penalty for each barrel knocked down.

CALF ROPING: While on her horse, the rider uses a lariat to catch the calf. She then gets off her horse, throws the calf to the ground, and uses what is called a pigging string to tie three of the calf's feet together. Her tie must hold for six seconds to qualify.

TEAM ROPING: This event involves a steer and two mounted cowgirls. The steer is released to get a head start. The header on the team ropes the steer around the horns or neck and turns the steer to the left. On the other side is the heeler of the team, who ropes the steer around the back legs.

To learn all that a horse could teach,
was a world of knowledge,
but only a beginning....
Look into a horse's eye and you instantly know
if you can trust him.

MARY O'HARA

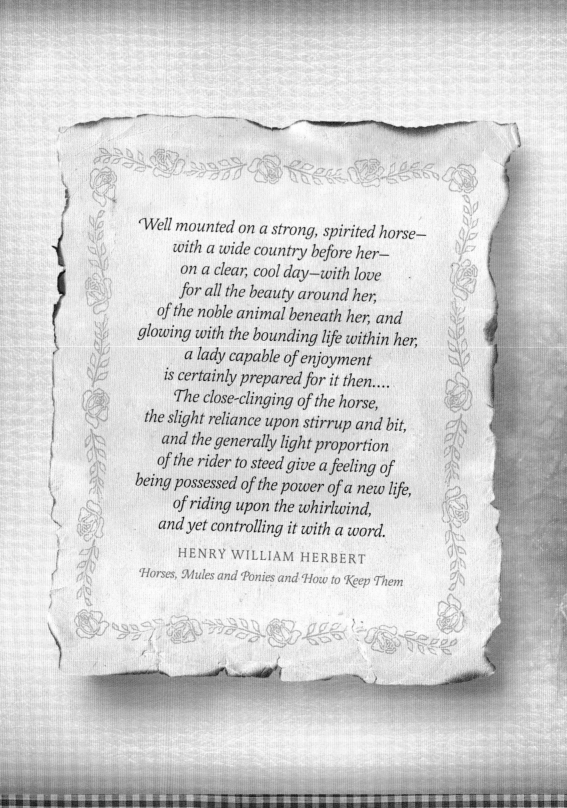

Well mounted on a strong, spirited horse—
with a wide country before her—
on a clear, cool day—with love
for all the beauty around her,
of the noble animal beneath her, and
glowing with the bounding life within her,
a lady capable of enjoyment
is certainly prepared for it then....
The close-clinging of the horse,
the slight reliance upon stirrup and bit,
and the generally light proportion
of the rider to steed give a feeling of
being possessed of the power of a new life,
of riding upon the whirlwind,
and yet controlling it with a word.

HENRY WILLIAM HERBERT
Horses, Mules and Ponies and How to Keep Them

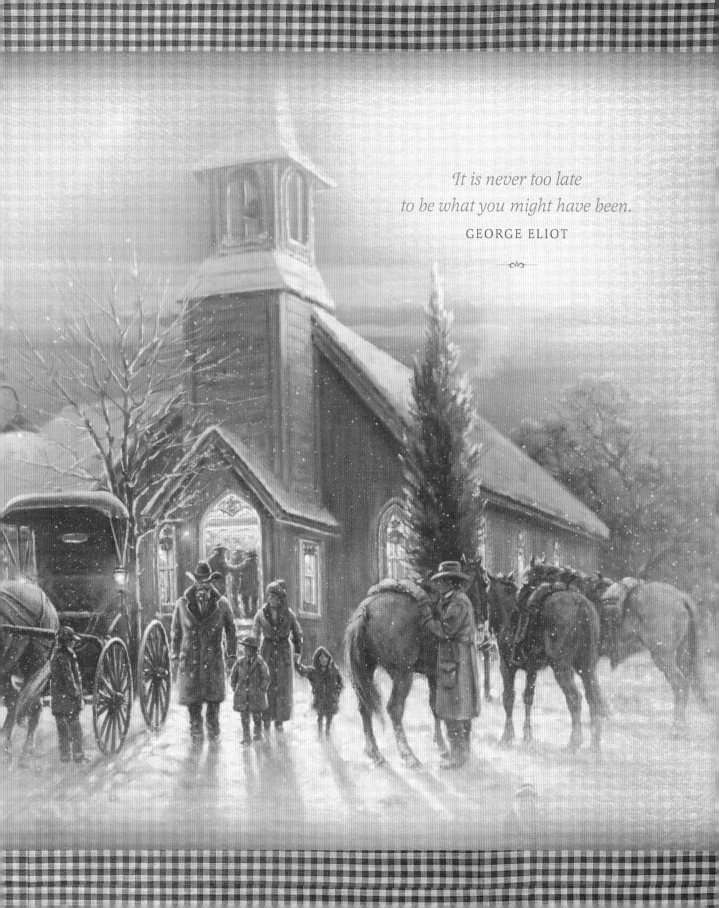

It is never too late
to be what you might have been.
GEORGE ELIOT